IMAGES
of America

NEW BRIGHTON

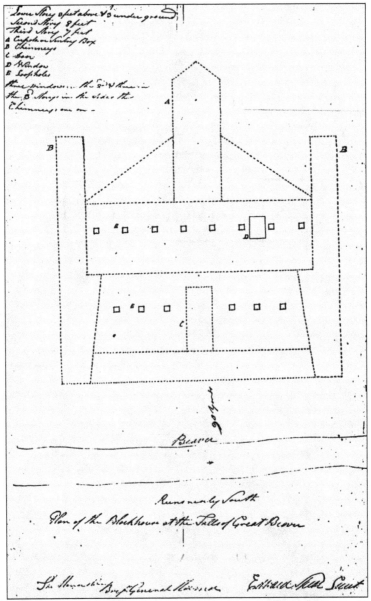

This blockhouse sketch was drawn by Lt. Edward Spears for Col. Josiah Harmar in 1788. Logs from the demolished Fort McIntosh were floated up the Beaver River to build the two-story blockhouse in present-day New Brighton. According to archival records, Lieutenant Spears hired local trader William Wilson to put a roof on the building. The blockhouse was abandoned in 1793. (Courtesy Clements Library, University of Michigan.)

ON THE COVER: The citizens of New Brighton put on a first-class weeklong centennial celebration in 1938 that ended with an afternoon parade. Standard Horse Nail employees show off their float in front of the company headquarters. It was one of the finest floats in the parade and was pulled by two teams of horses from Hyllmede Farm. (Courtesy Standard Horse Nail.)

IMAGES
of America

NEW BRIGHTON

Karen Helbling

ARCADIA
PUBLISHING

Published by Arcadia Publishing
Charleston, South Carolina

Library of Congress Control Number: 2012944935

For all general information, please contact Arcadia Publishing:
Telephone 843-853-2070
Fax 843-853-0044
E-mail sales@arcadiapublishing.com
For customer service and orders:
Toll-Free 1-888-313-2665

Visit us on the Internet at www.arcadiapublishing.com

*In memory of Edna Kramer McPherson, who started me on my
journey to becoming a steward of New Brighton history.*

CONTENTS

ACKNOWLEDGMENTS

In compiling this book, I am grateful to all the residents and school alumni who dug through old family albums searching for long-forgotten images of New Brighton.

And special thanks to my dear friend Sarah Lowe Eiler for sharing her 94 years of knowledge and her collection of Daugherty Township photographs. She was always there to answer any questions I had about the township or the town itself, for which I am extremely grateful.

I would like to thank the Beaver County Genealogical and History Center (BCGHC), and the Beaver County Historical Research and Landmarks Foundation (BCHRLF) for sharing their photographs. I would also like to acknowledge YMCA director Bill Parise for making available the vast number of historical images and files from the organization that were used in this publication.

Finally, I would like to thank my family, especially my brother Jerry, whose constant encouragement kept me focused on this project.

Unless otherwise noted, all photographs in this book are courtesy of the author.

INTRODUCTION

New Brighton is situated on the east bank of the Beaver River, about 30 miles northwest of Pittsburgh. In 1788, Col. Josiah Harmer and his troops from Fort McIntosh were ordered by an Act of Congress to build a blockhouse on present-day Third Avenue just below Fourteenth Street. At that time, it was the most advanced position held by the United States against the Indian tribes of the Ohio territory. When the blockhouse was abandoned in 1793, settlers began moving into the area.

John Wolf built and operated a flourmill near the old Tenth Street bridge in 1799. It was one of the first gristmills north of the Ohio River and was in operation until 1832.

A large financial boom came to the town in the 1830s when a branch of the United States Bank was located here. Merchants were encouraged to take out loans to improve their properties and townspeople were able to borrow money. With money flowing, the community was given the necessary financial security to make it thrive.

Ground was broken for the Beaver Division of the Pennsylvania Canal on July 28, 1831. The canal provided the needed transportation to get goods and supplies in and out of town. It was not long before businesses and manufacturers were recording huge profits.

By 1836, what once was a dense wilderness started to look like and take on the personality of a successful, quaint, and friendly community. The town's three sawmills were working shifts around the clock to keep up with the demand for lumber. At this time, the community had about 100 dwellings and a population of 900.

The town took a huge financial hit during the panic of 1837 when the United States Bank closed. Many merchants and residents faced high debts that they were unable to pay. But businessmen who were not affected by financial problems reinvested heavily in the town to help rebound the economy.

New Brighton was incorporated in June 1838. William Blanchard was appointed burgess and Francis Houlette was named tax collector and high constable. Council members were president W.H. Chamberlain, James Erwin, Levi McConnel, Septimus Dunlap, Charles Lukens, Isiah Smith, and secretary and treasurer Hamilton Hoopes.

When the Pennsylvania Railroad laid tracks through the town in 1853, immigrants traveled on it in search of employment. Businesses and manufacturers benefited by having skilled laborers, and employees were rewarded with higher than normal wages.

With the influx of people, grocery and drug stores, livery stables, hardware stores, and other mom-and-pop establishments were built around town to accommodate residents. Vendors who could not afford a storefront sold milk, groceries, fruits, vegetables, and household items from horse-drawn carts.

Author and journalist Sarah Jane Clarke wrote under the penname Grace Greenwood. Although she was born in New York, Clarke always felt that New Brighton was her home. In 1853, she wrote, "Our village is in a green and quiet valley and its pleasant society is a favorite summer resort for many of the citizens of Pittsburg and Cincinnati."

7

New Brighton played a major role in Civil War history. Company C, 63rd Pennsylvania Volunteers, and Company H, 9th Pennsylvania Reserves, were organized here. While the men were sent to fight in battles at Antietam, Gettysburg, and the Battle of the Wilderness, the women were busy sewing uniforms and making bandages in a room at the Fifth Avenue Methodist Church.

A Provo-Marshall's headquarters for the enlistment and examination of solders was set up in the former Anderson Building on Third Avenue and Eleventh Street. New Brighton native Capt. John Cuthbertson was wounded on June 30, 1862, at the battle of White Oak Swamp. When he returned home, he was appointed commanding officer of the post. Accommodations for the more than 3,000 soldiers who passed through the headquarters were in two barracks, one on the west side of Third Avenue near Twelfth Street and the other on Fourth Avenue just south of Eleventh Street, where a back room was turned into a jail to imprison deserters.

Company B, organized as a unit of the Pennsylvania National Guard in 1879, was under the command of Capt. Joseph Dewhirst. The company was mustered into service in May 1898. The regiment was redesignated as Company B, 110th Infantry, 28th Division, in 1917. It is the oldest division-sized unit in the armed forces of the United States.

While New Brighton prospered for many years, there were also hard times. Floods hit the town in 1832, 1884, 1907, 1913, and 1936. Each flood brought different challenges, but the town pulled together and rebuilt into an even stronger community each time. Factories with plants along Blockhouse Run felt the rage of the water every time a strong storm came in. At times, the usually quiet run would turn into a raging river, flooding nearby factories and homes.

One of New Brighton's earliest educational facilities was Miss Curtis' School for Girls, in the red brick building at 1305–1307 Third Avenue. The Brighton Academy, conducted by Rev. James Irvine, and the New Brighton High School, operated by Samuel Coulter, were both schools for boys that opened in 1851.

The Ladies Seminary opened in the old Water Cure building with Rev. John Davis as headmaster in 1853. Years later, the building was razed and the Central School was built on the same lot. Over the years, Central served as a high school, a junior high school, and an elementary school. Other elementary schools included First Ward, Third Ward, Fourth Ward, and Kenwood School.

The high school on Allegheny Street opened in the 1921–1922 school term. The facility housed students for 51 years before closing its doors in 1973. Today, the public school complex is on Forty-third Street in Pulaski Township and houses an elementary school, a high school, a theater, administrative offices, and a swimming pool. The New Brighton Middle School is on Penn Avenue.

One of the most popular amusement parks in the county, Junction Park, was on lower Third Avenue. It was founded by the Beaver County Traction Company and entertained visitors for more than 30 years. Older residents were often heard reminiscing about the elaborate Beaver County fairs held there in the early 1900s, or remembering spending the day on the amusement rides. When the park was in its heyday, it featured a first-class figure-eight roller coaster. Nothing remains of Junction Park today.

The 132-year-old Merrick Art Gallery, founded by Edward Dempster Merrick, is New Brighton's most valuable treasure. Each year, thousands of visitors stop by to view the permanent collection or attend special exhibits. The gallery offers summer outdoor concerts, summer art camp, and other art-related workshops.

The Beaver County YMCA has been a mainstay in New Brighton since 1889. Its deep-rooted dedication to the youth of the community is unsurpassed by any other organization. Today, the YMCA building, at 2236 Third Avenue, offers an up-to-date facility the whole family can enjoy.

Businesses that have helped the downtown area recapture some of its early charm are Waffles INCaffeinated, Hallowed Grounds, and the Yorktowne Shoppe. All are housed in original 19th-century structures and bring back the ambience of a simpler time and place.

One
MANUFACTURING

This photograph looks toward New Brighton from the Alum Rocks in 1907. The three-story brick building on the left, at 412 Second Avenue, was owned by David Love under the firm name D. Love and Company. The factory employed more than 30 workers, who made rugs out of old carpets. The business expanded into carpet cleaning and Love opened a furniture upholstering store at 514 Third Avenue in 1908.

David Townsend built the flourmill above on the bank of the Beaver River near present-day Fifth Street in 1828. The same year, he built a dam across the river to provide the waterpower needed to operate the facilities. Townsend sold the property to J.W. Wilson, who ran the mill successfully for many years until 1842, when he turned the business over to his son, Wade Wilson, who operated the mill until 1877. Below is the dam that powered the flourmill when the Pennsylvania Canal was completed and power was secured in exchange for granting the canal commissioners access to a right-of-way over Wilson's land. (Above, courtesy Vera Herr; below, courtesy Kathy Perenovich.)

Robert Townsend built the factory above on the west bank of the Beaver River at Fallston in 1828. His son, William Townsend, was taken on as a partner in 1840 when the firm became known as R. Townsend and Company. When Pittsburgh's Sixth Street Bridge was built in 1859, Townsend wire was used in the cables. The business incorporated as the C.C. and E.P. Townsend Company in 1905. The company grew to be an important supplier to the world's aircraft, automobile, railroad, and construction industries, as well as to the military. The Fallston plant covered more than five acres and was closed in the 1970s. The image below shows the devastation from the fire that struck the plant in 1915, resulting in 250 people losing their jobs. The two-hour blaze destroyed half of the original factory and the damages exceeded $100,000.

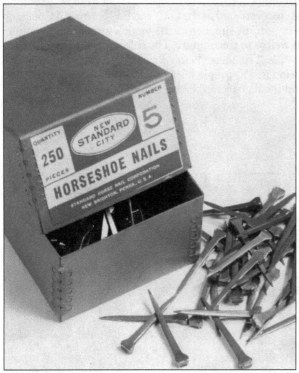

Charles Merrick and Job Whysall established Standard Horse Nail Works in Fallston in 1872. Erastus Pierce later joined the company when Whysall left to pursue other business ventures. Merrick and Pierce used their inventive genius to perfect a new hot-forging method for making horse nails in the late 1870s. After a fire destroyed the factory in 1885, Merrick built a new facility on Fifth Avenue in New Brighton. The employees above operate the machines used to manufacture gib keys, woodruff keys, machine keys, cotter pins, and taper pins. Today, the Merrick family operates the factory, with Robert S. Merrick Jr. as president and Ryan Merrick as vice president of operations. At left is a box of the nails manufactured under the Stanho brand. In the 1960s, the company stopped manufacturing horse nails and concentrated on fastening products. (Both, courtesy Standard Horse Nail.)

This undated photograph shows Standard Horse Nail Corporation salesmen, from left to right, (first row) Joe Koomar, Keith Anderson, Edward Brown, G. Blair Sheers, and J.D. Brubaker; (second row) W.S. Gardner Jr., William Wurzel, Ervin Feiler, W.C. Sheers, Robert Wyatt, company president Robert S. Merrick, Roger Javens, Mark Vosler, Harvey Cowan, and Raymond Cox. (Courtesy Standard Horse Nail.)

This photograph, taken from Patterson Heights in 1905, shows the downtown business section and the factories along the east bank of the Beaver River. While having the factories along the river was convenient and cost-effective for the manufacturers, they also had to deal with flooding every time a severe storm hit the town.

George W. and William D. Sherwood bought property along Blockhouse Run, which was rich in Kittanning clay, in 1878. A year later, they completed a small brick building, acquired a kiln, and formed Sherwood Brothers pottery. The pottery was known for its distinctive quality and style. The Kittanning clay was mixed with imported clays of a higher grade and used to manufacture light-glazed and dark-glazed Bristol and decorated ware. Accomplished artists did all the lettering. In 1888, the company listed 110 employees and sales of $100,000 annually. The Sherwood finish glaze gave each piece a durable surface. The image at left is a page from an 1889 catalog. Other wares included butter jars, hot water bottles, match scratchers and saucers, gold banded teapots, pitchers, jugs of all shapes and sizes, ginger beer bottles, mugs, steins, bowls, and coffee pots. The pottery closed in 1948.

The Pittsburgh Wallpaper Company started with one machine in a small factory in Pittsburgh before buying a factory in New Brighton in 1900. The firm occupied two buildings, each two stories high and 400 feet long, and employed more than 450 workers. The capacity of the works at this time was 200,000 rolls annually. In the fall of 1901, a four-story building was erected with a steel bridge connecting two of the buildings. It was the largest factory of its kind in point of capacity in the country at the time. By 1902, the plant operated 19 machines, had 25 traveling salesmen throughout the country, and produced more than 15 million rolls a year, selling for 40¢ a roll. On October 26, 1915, a fire (below) caused over $200,000 in damages and left 650 workers unemployed, devastating the business.

Edward Dawes and William Myler moved from Pittsburgh to New Brighton in 1897. They constructed a six-story building on Allegheny Street at Grove Avenue. The Hollow Ware Works enameled ironware and pump cylinders. The company became Standard Sanitary Manufacturing in 1900. A three-story enameling department was built in 1907 opposite the original warehouse. A steel bridge connected the new building with the original structure on the other side of Allegheny Street. When the company expanded to enameling bathtubs, the business boomed. The trade card above was used as advertising in 1907. Below is an undated photograph of the Dawes and Myler factory workers. Work-related accidents were numerous, with employees suffering from molten metal burns, crushed fingers, and smashed legs. Company records show that $30,000 a week in wages was paid out from 1908 to 1919. The plant closed in 1928.

This overview of the town was taken in 1909. The building on the riverbank in the center was used as an icehouse. Local meat merchant Fred Duerr owned the business. In the winter, blocks of ice were cut from the Beaver River and stored in the icehouse for many months. A fleet of four wagons was used to deliver the ice to households throughout town.

The Pittsburgh Clay Manufacturing Company was better known as the Elverson, Sherwood, and Barker pottery. The plant covered five acres on Blockhouse Run. The company invented and produced the first self-sealing fruit jars, which are still found in antique stores today. Dr. H.S. McConnel, one of New Brighton's best-known physicians, was president of the company in the early 1900s.

John P. O'Leary Sr. and Thomas Woolaway founded Tuscarora Plastics in 1962. The corporate headquarters and its first plant were on Fifth Avenue. Tuscarora Plastics was the nation's largest manufacturer of molded foam packaging. The company acquired similar small businesses that made plastic foam packing, and by 1980, it was producing polystyrene foam at a dozen locations. During the Gulf War, the company shipped the sensitive nose cones of the Patriot air-defense missiles in large, expandable bead-shaped polystyrene packages. The corporate offices are seen above after being untouched by a fire on February 4, 1970. The image below shows the destruction from the massive fire to the rear of the building that housed the manufacturing plant. Tuscarora Plastics, under the name and management of the Tegrant Corporation, closed in 2009. (Both, courtesy Gary Borland.)

Two

COMMERCE

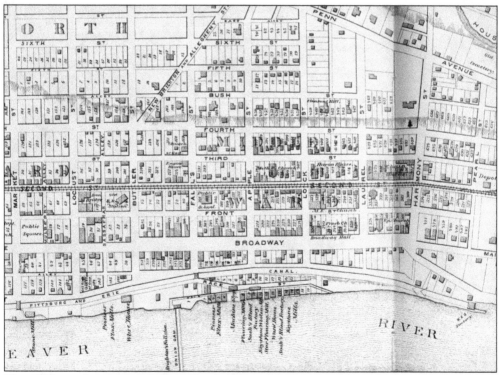

This 1876 map shows some of the old landmarks and the names of the early town streets. Around 1900, the streets were renamed and the main thoroughfare, Broadway, became Third Avenue. Second Street, known as Railroad Street by the locals, is where the train tracks were first laid in 1853. The canal and race is visible at the bottom of this map. (Survey map by J.A. Caldwell.)

PHOTOGRAPHERS,

227 BROADWAY,

NEW BRIGHTON, PA.

The McClain brothers' photography studio was located on a boat near the canal bridge in the early years of the business. In the 1870s, they moved the studio to 227 Broadway. After the brothers dissolved their partnership in 1877, John McClain took on George Bert, who was well known for his oil and crayon portraits, as a partner. When McClain retired around 1882, Bert took charge of the business.

J. Edgar Ryan established Brighton Dry Goods (right side, halfway down) at 900 Third Avenue with business partner Annie Bockey in 1899. At the time, the store employed nine clerks. Ryan became the sole proprietor in 1901, retaining Bockey as store buyer. The upper half of the building was sold to George Bestwick in 1909 as an investment. Ryan kept control of the lower levels, which housed his store and the Frishkorn Brothers grocery.

This 1909 photograph shows 1301 Third Avenue, the longtime home of John P. and Lydia Sherwood. The handsome brick residence contained 13 rooms, a bath, and a pantry. In 1917, the house was sold to their niece, Annie Rigby, who operated a boardinghouse until 1930. The Joseph J. Spratt and Brother Funeral Home was located here until 1947. (Courtesy J.J. Spratt Funeral Home.)

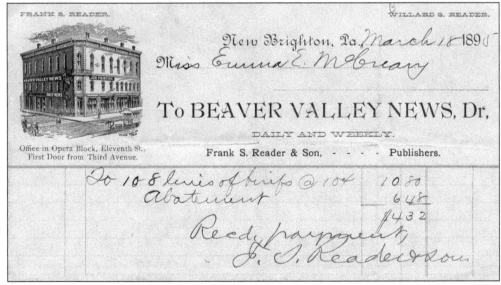

Frank S. Reader began publication of the first daily newspaper in the county, the *Beaver Valley News*, on February 4, 1883. Willard Reader worked at his father's office as an apprentice while attending Geneva College and became the reporter for New Brighton in 1889. When he turned 21 in 1892, he was admitted as a partner in the business and named city editor.

Roland L. Kenah (left side of doorway) owned and operated a drugstore and apothecary on Broadway—now the corner of Third Avenue and Ninth Street. The others in this photograph are, from left to right, his apprentice Francis W. Walker, and his children William H., Roland Jr., Charles, and Franklin (in baby carriage). The two young boys and the man leaning against the hitching post are unidentified. (Courtesy Bill Edwards.)

BUY
HORACE WATERS & CO.'S
CELEBRATED PIANOS & ORGANS
FROM D. R. Magaw, Gen'l. Ag't.
NEW BRIGHTON, PA.

D.R. Magaw ran a successful shoe store in the opera house block from 1872 to 1890. The enterprising entrepreneur became an agent for the Horace Waters and Company's piano and organ line. Magaw purchased a Walters piano and hired local pianist Mary Jackson to serenade patrons every Friday and Saturday night as they shopped. The venture paid off and his profits were used to bankroll a loan business in Pittsburgh.

22

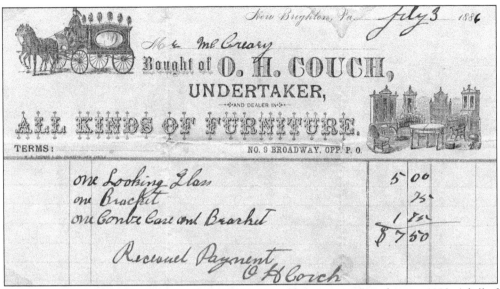

New Brighton, Pa. July 3 1886

Mr. McCreary

Bought of O. H. COUCH,

UNDERTAKER,

AND DEALER IN

ALL KINDS OF FURNITURE.

TERMS: NO. 9 BROADWAY, OPP. P. O.

one Looking Glass	5 00
one Bracket	75
one Centre Case and Bracket	1 75
	$ 7 50

Received Payment
O H Couch

O.H. Couch located his furniture and undertaking establishment on Broadway in 1883. A bill of sale from 1886 is seen here. After Couch died in 1908, his son Nathan, who had his own undertaker business, took over his father's furniture store. By February 1909, Nathan Couch realized he could no longer run two businesses and discontinued his father's furniture store, renting the storeroom to the Hostine Company.

The Ewing brothers, James, Edgar, Homer, and Frank (seen here) established the Ewing Brothers clothing store at 1001 Third Avenue in 1890. The spacious store was known for its handsome displays of superior-quality suits, shirts, and accessories for men and boys at reasonable prices. The business was a huge success and a second store opened in nearby Rochester. (Courtesy BCHRLF.)

Above, hundreds gather to attend a play at the Broadway Hall Company in the Opera House at 106 Broadway. B.B. Chamberlin, A.D. Gilliland, E.B. Thompson, and W.W. Irvin incorporated the company on March 29, 1872. The upper levels of the building are where the public enjoyed lectures, exhibitions, operas, and concerts. A fire completely destroyed the third floor and severely damaged the lower floors in February 1899. Other establishments were also damaged, including the G.W. Carey shoe store, William Graham's mercantile, A.D. Gilliland dry goods, Emil Stucky's drugstore, H.L. Schweppe's drugstore, the armory of Company A, and the office of the *Beaver Valley News*. Below is a trade card from the Gilliland mercantile that was tucked into the owner's pocket shortly before the fire. The lower two floors were rebuilt and the building still stands today at the corner of Third Avenue and Eleventh Street.

Stuart Magee immigrated to the United States from Ireland in 1872. In the late 1890s, he started a grocery store at 1000 Eleventh Street. He was a dealer in groceries, provisions, flour, feed, dry goods, and notions. In the summer months, Magee kept a small antique cart in front of the store. Emily Templeton, a local florist, filled the cart daily with fresh flowers for customers to purchase. The inside of the store is seen below. If a customer wanted homegrown produce, Magee's grocery was the perfect place to shop. When in season, local farmers delivered pecks of handpicked apples, peaches, plums, tomatoes, peppers, and green beans every day. After Magee's death, his wife, Mary, sold the business to Louis Madory and G.C. Hilpert in 1925. (Both, courtesy BCHRLF.)

This photograph looks at Broadway and Falls Street in the early 1870s, when Broadway (now Third Avenue) was still a dirt thoroughfare. Dr. Alfred M. Whisler moved his dental practice to the second floor above the J.B. Noble Drug Store in 1867. The next building (left) housed a hardware store operated by longtime merchant George W. Martsolf.

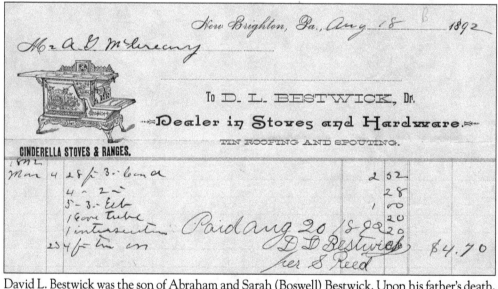

David L. Bestwick was the son of Abraham and Sarah (Boswell) Bestwick. Upon his father's death, David took charge of the Bestwick Hardware store on Broadway. This invoice, dated August 1892, shows that Bestwick was also a supplier of Cinderella stoves and ranges. He continued to run the business successfully for a few years before closing it and moving his family to Sebring, Ohio.

Nicholas Wurzel was born in 1823 in Seligenstädt, Germany. He came to the United States in 1844 and married Elizabeth Winters on May 6, 1851. The Wurzel family is seen above, from left to right, (first row) John W. Wurzel, Christopher U. Wurzel, Theresa Wurzel Ruff, and Frank H. Wurzel; (second row) Agnes Wurzel Dennis, Nicholas Wurzel Jr., Elizabeth Winter Wurzel (wife of Nicholas), Nicholas Wurzel Sr., and Anna Mary Wurzel Husser; (third row) George Wurzel, Samuel Wurzel, Magdalena Wurzel, Henry Wurzel, Mary Philamina Wurzel Garber, Edward Wurzel, and Elizabeth Wurzel Barker. At right, from left to right, are Heinrich Wurzel, Nicholas Wurzel Sr., unidentified, and Elizabeth Winter Wurzel in front of the store at the corner of Third Avenue and Eleventh Street. Floors Galore operates from the building today. (Both, courtesy John Cater.)

August Madory moved to Beaver County in 1889. He later purchased a grocery store at 1031 Third Avenue. His wife, Emma, died in 1908 at the age of 38, leaving him with a business and eight children. Bertha Flinner, Esther Madory, and Louis Madory were clerks. When August died, his children assumed responsibility for the store and continued running it in the same location until 1925.

Fanny Makovicka owned and operated a tobacco shop and lunchroom (pictured) at 1136 Third Avenue in the 1920s. Glass display cases held the Tom Keene brand of cigars, which sold for 5¢ each. Lunch patrons could purchase a bowl of soup, a sandwich, and a drink for 25¢. Her husband, Eugene, operated a tailor shop out of their apartment above the store. (Courtesy BCHRLF.)

Charles F. Kramer purchased the newsstand of G.W. Williams in February 1900 and retained Williams's assistant, Caroline Carey. Kramer later built and moved his successful business to 919 Third Avenue. John G. McCrory leased the storefront (left) and opened one of his popular 5 and 10¢ stores. The store typically sold fabrics, penny candy, toys, shoes, clothing, housewares, and cosmetics.

This 1910 photograph shows the improvements made to Third Avenue, after the once-dirt road was paved with bricks. David and Lena Gold were the longtime office managers for the American Express Company and Western Union Telegraph and Cable offices (left).

This photograph shows the success of the downtown business district in 1908 on a typical Saturday afternoon. The crowd on the left waits to enter the grand opening of the Avenue Theater. Patrons were treated to a fun-filled afternoon of vaudeville and moving pictures. Manager Harry Murden gave everyone who attended the opening day showings a coupon good for one free weekday performance.

Milo F. Wilson started his grocery store at 901 Third Avenue (far left) in 1895. By 1902, he had built up a house-to-house delivery service selling Elgrin Creamery butter and butterine. The weekly output to his 8,000 regular customers was more than 9,000 pounds. A fleet of 10 wagons delivered the butter products throughout Beaver County, Ohio, and West Virginia. Wilson's nickname was the "Butter Man of Yesterday."

Philip and Magdalene Ondrusek opened their first grocery at 1312 Allegheny Street in the early 1900s. Later, they purchased a storefront at 901 Penn Avenue. The butchers above worked at this location, called the Economy Food Market. A second location opened later at 818 Third Avenue. When the junior high school was built, the Penn Avenue store closed. In the 1940s, a store opened on Fifth Avenue and Ninth Street. The Economy had fresh strawberries flown in daily on TWA flights from California in the early 1960s. This marked the first time in the tri-state area that strawberries were on the grocer's shelf within eight hours of being picked. The Ondrusek family ran the Economy Supermarket until 1985, when the family-owned corporation was dissolved. (Courtesy Mimi Ondrusek.)

The 1941 YMCA basketball champions were sponsored by the Economy Food Market. (Courtesy YMCA.)

A passenger waits to get on the trolley at the corner of Third Avenue and Ninth Street in the summer of 1907. The building on the right, at 825 Third Avenue, housed Harvey's Nickelodeon. The nickelodeon was on the first floor and bowling and billiard rooms were on the upper floors. Both successful businesses were owned and operated by Edward Harvey for many years.

The Masonic Building (left) was formally opened on May 2, 1907, at a cost of $40,000. A grand opening luncheon was served to 1,500 people in the banquet hall. Sepps' Orchestra provided music. Tenants of the building included Pane and Covert Market, James B. Edgar Funeral Home, and the Bachelor Club. C.L. Lewin and M. Scaffel operated the Empire Theater. The building burned twice and was rebuilt.

The New Brighton Hotel, later named the Merrick House, was built by the Brighton House Company on Broadway in 1836. When the panic of 1837 struck, the two lower levels were used as a hotel and the upper levels were leased by Marcus Gould to raise silkworms. In 1850, the property was sold to Silas Merrick, John Miner, and Edward Hoopes. On October 5, 1855, the hotel was destroyed by fire.

William Keyser built the Keyser House, a first-class hotel, on Pearl Street in 1877. Rooms rented for $2 a day at the time. William Boyle managed the hotel for several years before purchasing the business in 1915. Boyle called his establishment the Clyde House. Other proprietors over the years included James Glasson, Frank Cashbaugh, and William Leckemby. The hotel was completely destroyed by fire in 1976.

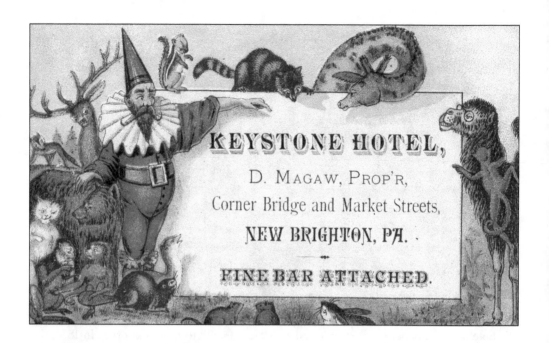

David Magaw was the proprietor of the Keystone Hotel, opposite Townsend Park, in 1869. It contained 20 elaborately furnished rooms, offices, two parlors, a dining room, and a bar. John Risinger was a popular hostler in the early years. In September 1870, a chambermaid found Nellie Lathom, of Chicago, stabbed to death in her bed. Hours later, a drifter named Jonathan Watterson was charged with her murder. Magaw sold the business to Henry L. Stuber in 1892 and it became known as the Park Hotel. It is seen below after Stuber sold the hotel to Sidney Cook in 1904. Other proprietors included Robert Wintersgill, Robert Fleming, and D. Weber. Samuel Wurzel tended the hotel bar for many years. The frame building, at what is now Third Avenue and Sixth Street, was razed in 1938.

The Hotel Brighton was located at the corner of Falls and Railroad Streets. The three-story brick building that housed the first public school was renovated into a handsome hotel with 30 rooms, a formal dining room, and a parlor where guests could mingle. In the summer, large shade trees kept guests cool as they sipped lemonade on the porch that surrounded the building. James. L. Mayhew was the popular proprietor.

Construction on the Sourbeck Hotel began in 1850, but before it was completed, a fire destroyed the building. After it was rebuilt in 1851, the Sourbeck became one of the most popular hotels in town. Daniel and Eliza Sourbeck owned the hotel for many years before selling it to Major Scott before 1870. This is a page from an original hotel registry dated 1889, when Scott was still the proprietor.

The Kenwood Hotel was on Third Avenue at Fifth Street. The three-story building, the former Sourbeck Hotel, was built in 1851. Samuel Gallagher purchased the 20-room structure in 1897 and renamed it the Kenwood Hotel. The hotel was complete with a dining room and a well-stocked bar. Electric lights and baths were added in 1901 after an electric light plant was installed in the basement. Robert Glenn, the night clerk, was responsible for keeping the engine clean and in good running order. Other proprietors included James Cain, R.M. Zang, Max Klein, and Mary Seybert. Below, curious onlookers gather to watch firefighters battle a fire at the 125-year-old Kenwood Hotel on August 13, 1976. The wooden building had been vacant for two years and was a total loss. The structure was razed in 1977.

Sarah and Sallie Molter, the twin daughters of Frank and Edith Molter, are seen here on the porch of their home at 1415 Fourth Avenue. Molter saw the large home as an asset, and in the early 1900s, he opened it as a boardinghouse. The rooms, which guests could rent by the week or the month, included a comfortable bed and a small desk and chair. A hearty breakfast started the day and another home-cooked meal awaited them every evening. For an additional fee, boarders could request laundry service or have their room cleaned. The Molter's six children, Howard C., Estella B., Oliver J., Frank D., and the twins, helped their mother with the daily chores involved with the business. Below, Edith relaxes in the beautifully decorated parlor, where boarders would gather to get the news of the day.

The 900 block of Third Avenue is seen here in the 1960s. Puritan Drug (left) was owned by Irwin and Doris Clateman for 39 years. Leon Panella, Harry Davis, and Pete Antinopolis were longtime pharmacists at Puritan. Rite Aid purchased the business in 1989, and Panella and Davis opened a drugstore on Ninth Street. Today, Davis owns Brighton Health Mart Pharmacy on Fifth Avenue.

George's Place, on the corner of Third Avenue and Strawberry Alley, was owned and operated by George and Christine Straile. The front half of the building was used as a grocery store and featured a soda fountain while a bar at the back served beer only. The second floor was the family living quarters. (Courtesy Eleanor Straile Cabana.)

Sing Lee Laundry (above, left) was located at 805 Third Avenue. Lee signed a five-year lease in 1901 with Addison Wilson, the proprietor of the building. Wilson violated the lease when he sold the building to Charles Davis in 1903 and put all of Lee's belongings in the street. Lee sued Wilson for damages in a Pittsburgh court and won a $250 settlement. The Ming Laundry (above, right) was owned and operated by Klong Kee. The same business block is seen below in the 1960s. The store on the left was Lee Johnson Boys' Wear for many years, with Brighton Sporting Goods next door. The building was owned by the Autenreith family for many years. These structures in the 800 block of downtown were purchased by the Citizens Economic Development Corporation and later torn down to make room for a Rite Aid.

Wade and Edith Lemmon opened Lemmon's Market in 1936 at 119 Mercer Road. In the beginning, customers either came in person or phoned in their orders to be delivered. The store housed the first frozen-food case in town. The Lemmon children, Lois, Don, Joan, Tom, and Nancy, worked at the market, which served the residents of Oak Hill for 54 years. In 1990, Edith sold to Charles and Ross Kemp.

Otto R. McNutt moved to New Brighton from Kentucky in 1901 and worked for the Martsolf brothers, who were contractors and builders, for seven years. He then went into business for himself, purchasing Fred McDanel's lumberyard at Sixth Avenue and Eleventh Street, where the post office is today. This thermometer was given to customers as a company promotion. (Courtesy Charlene McNutt.)

Rev. Harriet Christner established the Beaver Valley Gospel Tabernacle on February 12, 1939. In 1944, the tabernacle moved to the second floor of 1036 Third Avenue. Christner's Christian Bookstore (left) was established on the main floor, with family living quarters on the upper floor. Christner and her daughter Jean operated the bookstore until October 20, 1963, when a fire destroyed the entire building.

Hundreds of people gathered on Broadway between Apple and Lock Streets to watch one of the many New Brighton merchants' parades held in the early 1900s. Bands entertained the crowds as fleets of horse-drawn wagons advertising various businesses paraded throughout the town. The New Brighton Ohio Mineral Water Company wagon (center) was one of seven that delivered their products to merchants around the county.

Sammy Cardosi stands in the doorway of the barbershop he opened on Third Avenue at Tenth Street in July 1951. He was at this location for 48 years before relocating the shop to the 700 block of Third Avenue. The shop was a meeting place for regular customers, who would stop by in between haircuts to catch up on the news of the day. (Courtesy Sammy Cardosi.)

Identical twins Thomas and David Helbling opened a soft-serve ice cream business in a small stand called Twin Kiss on Rochester Road on June 27, 1958. Additions were built around the stand until it was transformed into the restaurant seen here in 1969. Twin Kiss was one of the first establishments to serve root beer in frosty mugs. (Courtesy Thomas and Regina Helbling.)

Above, John M. Spratt (left) and James P. Spratt walk in front of the J.J. Spratt Funeral Home on Third Avenue. The business, started by their father, Joseph J. Spratt, moved to this location when their widowed mother, Julia (Mack) Spratt, bought the home from Carl and Betty Brosh in 1948. That was the beginning of the J. Spratt Funeral Home. Julia died in March 1957, leaving the business to her sons. It then became the J.J. Spratt Funeral Home. The family business continues today under supervisor and funeral director Jay Daniel Spratt. Below, in March 1928, a Clark vault was disinterred in Grove Cemetery. The casket was found to be in perfect condition, although the grave showed evidence of having been very wet. This proved that there was no better protection than that afforded by the vault. (Both, courtesy J.J. Spratt Funeral Home.)

When Elmer Horner operated a service station and store on Marion Hill Road in the 1930s, gas was still 10¢ a gallon. The well-stocked store sold penny candy, eggs, bread, and other necessities. In those days, it was not unusual for a filling station to sell more than one brand of gasoline and oil. In 1955, the station became a full-service Ashland dealer. (Courtesy Thomas Helbling.)

In 1955, a fire devastated the George E. Gordon distributors on upper Third Avenue near Seventh Street. The fire consumed the business and destroyed the living quarters on the second floor. The building was not occupied at the time of the fire but was a total loss. However, firefighters were able to contain the flames before they spread to Lawrence Heating (left).

Three
TRANSPORTATION

Charles Hayward (left) and Robert McClymonds take time to pose for a photograph in early 1900. McClymonds's first job with the trolley company was driving extra horses to his father, William, who was a driver on the horse-drawn railway line. When buses replaced the streetcars, McClymonds went from a trolley operator to a bus driver and operated a cross-town bus between New Brighton and Beaver Falls into his 70s.

Wooden packet boats like the *Jack Boyle* were familiar sights in the heyday of the canals. George Bannon (above, left) and Samuel McDanel (right) pose on the boat at Blount's Lock in 1870. The town had four single locks, Blount's at Tenth Street, Buck's Woods at Eleventh Street, Stone Cut at Thirteenth Street, and Van Lear's at Fourteenth Street. Boats were pulled through the canal by a team of mules, who walked along a towpath beside the water. The canal office, where patrons paid tolls or transacted business, stood on the east side of the canal near the back of what is now First National Bank. On the west side of the canal was a drydock where boats were repaired. Below, a packet boat carries passengers up the Beaver River in 1870. The only lock still visible today can be seen from the Fallston Bridge.

William McClymonds was drafted into the 101st Pennsylvania Infantry during the Civil War, serving three years before he was discharged in 1865. He became a trolley driver when streetcars were pulled with horses in the late 1880s. When electric trolleys were introduced, he became one of the first motormen for the Beaver Valley Traction Company. A highly respected pioneer in his field, McClymonds died on November 28, 1904.

The Beaver County Traction Company bought the Riverview Street Railway Company in 1891. Early drivers for the company were James Ross, William McClymonds, and James Boswell. Below, motormen Samuel Morgan (left) and Robert McClymonds show off an open-sided electric streetcar used to deliver mail in the 1890s. McClymonds was one of the operators on the final streetcar trip from Junction Park to Morado and back on August 10, 1937.

Above, a steam engine makes its daily run down Railroad Street in the 1850s. Trains had to stop at Butler Street to fill up with water pumped by horsepower from the canal. Accidents involving trains and townspeople were frequent, as shoppers heading to the business district had to cross the tracks. In 1852, council approved an ordinance that forbade engineers from exceeding eight miles per hour through town. Early railroad records show that Merrick, Hanna, and Company made wrought-iron passenger cars here in 1857. They are believed to have been the first metal railroad cars made in the United States. The image below shows Railroad Street between Lock and Apple Streets. The building in the back right was the Fifth Avenue Methodist Church. The railroad tracks were moved from Railroad Street to the bank of the Beaver River in 1926.

The Pennsylvania, Fort Wayne & Chicago Railroad passenger depot was at the corner of Railroad and Lock Streets, where the Merrick Art Gallery stands today. Inside the station, patrons could purchase tickets, get up-to-date train schedules, and arrange hotel stays. Waiting rooms provided a place for passengers to sit and talk with others about the news of the day. Station agents included John Reeves, M.S. Johns, Thomas Farley, J.W. Witherow, and R.E. Hoopes. The building on the far right housed a branch of the Ward and Mackey Company, makers of bread and crackers, which was headquartered in Pittsburgh. Only the best-grade ingredients went into their red, white, and blue–labeled Mother's Bread. The image below looks westward in August 1926 at the Kenwood Tower of the Pennsylvania Railroad, on the banks of the Beaver River.

Employees of the Beaver County Traction Company went on strike in 1899. This disturbance was the first in the company's history, leaving officials unprepared, and residents forced to find other modes of transportation. When the streets became overcrowded with horses and buggies, tempers flared. Police officers responded as minor skirmishes broke out around town. Workers posed for this photograph eight days after the strike began.

The Beaver Valley Motor Coach Company buses began replacing the streetcars in 1937. The company rolled out more than 50 modern motor coaches to handle passenger needs. The state highway department quickly moved to have the existing streetcar tracks removed and roads repaired for bus traffic. Fares remained between 10¢ and 15¢. Many trolley operators who became bus drivers are seen here.

Four

INSTITUTIONS

The Beaver Valley General Hospital built the Beaver Valley School of Nursing on Penn Avenue in 1922. The brick building cost $80,000 and had 45 dormitory rooms, a snack kitchen, a chapel, lounge rooms, and a science laboratory. One classroom was set up to simulate an operating room and another to simulate a hospital room. The school closed in the 1970s and the building was razed in April 2010. (Courtesy BCHRLF.)

The Bradford homestead was built at the corner of Broadway and Apple Street in 1846 and was razed in April 1900 to make room for a new post office. The handsome government building, with a price tag of $75,000, opened on March 28, 1902. The one-story stone, brick, and terra-cotta structure was 84 feet by 48 feet and 40 feet high. Broad marble steps led up to revolving doors opening into the vestibule, which was finished in Vermont red marble. Inside the side entrance was a 12-foot public corridor, wainscoted up 12 feet in red marble and finished in polished, quartered white oak. The lockboxes and general delivery, stamp, and carrier windows were all polished brass and beveled plate glass. There were 294 gas and electric lights throughout. There were two vaults, one opening into the main office and one into the money room. In the rear of the building was a small room for receiving mail from trains and streetcars. The large terra-cotta eagle graced the top of the building until it was razed in 1976.

In early 1900, Edward Dawes built a house at 1450 Third Avenue. In his will, he stated that the home should be used as a facility to care for elderly women run by a board of directors. Dawes Manor opened in 1913 and served the area for 89 years, closing its doors in 2002. Carol Weeber, then 88 years old, was the last resident at the manor.

Employees of the Beaver Valley General Hospital joined forces with the Beaver Valley School of Nursing students to create this float for the 125th anniversary parade held in June 1963. The nurses are wearing uniforms from the early 1900s. (Courtesy Gary Borland.)

The Beaver Valley School of Nursing presented the above students with their caps in the spring of 1947: from left to right, (first row) Fran McGaffick, Doris E. Greaves, and Norma Jean Downey; (second row) Genevieve Zahn, Jean Laughlin, and Ann Phillips; (third row) Jean Warner, Libby Hoit, and Sylvia Kushner. (Courtesy Doris Greaves Rexroad.)

The 1965 graduates of the Beaver Valley School of Nursing were, from left to right, (top row) Sydney Borland (valedictorian), Betty Rimbey (director of nursing), and Bonnie Bower; (second row) Thelma Cribbs, Nancy Coon, Judith Dobbs, and Cheryl Gidos; (third row) Gloria Kibler, Bonnie Layton, Carol Mains, and Sally Moore; (fourth row) Helen Rowe, Judith Shoff, Eleanor Snyder, and Janice West; (bottom row) Ilona Wright and Carol Yonata. (Courtesy Gary Borland.)

The Union National Bank, located on Broadway at Falls Street, was chartered on April 20, 1891, with a capital of $50,000. Charles M. Merrick was elected president and served in that capacity for many years. Other officers were vice president E. Autenreith, cashier Ernest Seiple, assistant cashier C.C. Keck, and messenger H.R. Boots. The board of directors included Merrick, J.F. Miner, John A. Jackson, Edward Blount, and Dr. W.C. Simpson.

The Beaver County Trust Company absorbed the old established banking company of Charles Barker and Company in 1901. That same year, it contracted R.B. McDanel and Son to build a new bank at 1024 Third Avenue. The handsome structure was completed in May 1902. Officers at that time were president Frederick G. Barker, vice president Charles Barker, treasurer George Davidson, and secretary Agnew Hice.

The interior of the Beaver County Trust Company on Third Avenue was as handsome as the terracotta trimmed outside. The above image shows the heavy oak and glass doors that brought patrons into the establishment. Teardrop-shaped chandeliers shipped in from England hung gracefully from the high ceiling. Beautiful hand-carved crown molding wrapped around the top of the room and across the ceiling. The bank was a state depository and handled trust estates aggregating more than $500,000 in 1904. Depositors knew their savings were secure in the state-of-the-art safe (left) behind the barred gate in the back of the bank. Another safe was housed in the basement. In the 1940s, the bank began offering customers the convenience of paying their electric and telephone bills there while tending to their regular banking needs.

Five

NOTABLE PEOPLE

This is one of artist and photographer Henry Noss's greatest novelties. The work, titled *Life Among the Fairies*, was completed around 1874. He often referred to it as the "Bouquet of Innocence" and it contains the portraits of his four oldest children and their cat. A monarch butterfly also feeds on a nearby flower. (Photograph by Henry Noss.)

Henry Noss moved to New Brighton in 1850. He was hired as a bellboy at the Merrick House and stayed in that position until 1855. Noss began his photography career in 1856 on the second floor of a small brick building on Railroad Street (now Fifth Avenue). After finding great success in the photography field, he moved his gallery above Billy Magee's grocery store on Broadway. Noss took this photograph in the 1880s and it illustrates how creative he was at marketing his

products outside the studio. He entertained passersby with an ambrotype display; no one could resist stopping and taking a look inside. Noss was in business at this location for more than 30 years and his fine quality photographs and stereoviews are still sought by collectors today. (Photograph by Henry Noss; courtesy BCHRLF.)

The famous "Musical Noss Family" included, from left to right, Mary, Flora, Bertha, Ferd, Henry, Lottie, and Frank. When they performed a rendition of the *Drummer of Shiloh* at the Opera House on Broadway, it got the attention of a New York agent who offered them a contract for a New England tour. They went on to become top entertainers in the industry and were in demand in the United States, Canada, Mexico, and throughout Europe. When their parents retired and moved back to the family home at 923 Sixth Avenue, the children billed themselves as the "Five Musical Nosses" (below) and became a vaudeville success in New York. Mary Noss, Henry's second wife, used her experience as a dressmaker to sew the costumes. The family retired in 1924.

Edward Dempster Merrick's boyhood dreams of becoming an artist finally came true at age 53. Not wanting to go to school, he had spent hours observing nature and painting what he saw. He bought the old railroad station, renovated it into an art gallery, and traveled to New York and Europe to purchase paintings for his collection. He made chestnut and rosewood boxes to surround the paintings and protect them from dust. Merrick was a tall gentleman whose light-blue eyes twinkled behind gold-rimmed glasses. Townspeople found him a little odd and did not fully understand him or his museum at the time. Every afternoon, with a butterfly net in hand, he walked to Oak Hill to gather specimens for the museum. After his death in 1911, his butterfly collection was given to the Smithsonian Institution. Merrick painted more than 220 paintings that he signed in a way that could not be copied. All of his own works mysteriously disappeared after his death. The gallery is filled with paintings purchased by Merrick and is the oldest operating museum in western Pennsylvania. (Courtesy Robert and Eva Mae Merrick.)

A group of academy-style paintings gathered by Edward Dempster Merrick from around the world are on exhibit at the Merrick Art Gallery on Eleventh Street. The piano above, originally located in the Merrick House, was played by legendary composer Stephen Foster and is displayed in the Eva Mae Merrick Music Room. The gallery is on the State and National Registers of Historic Places. (Courtesy Robert and Eva Mae Merrick.)

Sarah Jane Clarke (left) wrote poetry and stories about her life here under the *nom de plume* Grace Greenwood. In 1853, she married Leander Lippincott and they published *Little Pilgrim* magazine. Greenwood wrote for the *Saturday Evening Post*, the *New York Times*, and *Harper's Monthly*. She was the first female journalist allowed to cover political news on the floor of Congress. She also lectured and fought for women's rights.

This beautiful Queen Anne–style house, at 1435 Third Avenue, was built in 1894 for Frederick and Clara Merrick. The house, with seven bedrooms and three and a half bathrooms, was an exact copy of a house they fell in love with on a visit to Cape Cod. Local residents refer to the 5,000-square-foot, three-story house as "The Castle." Its architectural beauty, inside and out, is what makes it unique. The 21-foot-by-17-foot formal reception hall is seen below. The beautiful hand-carved mantels, gorgeous wooden coffered ceilings, and hardwood floors made the room even more inviting to guests. The grand oak staircase leads to a massive curved stained-glass window. (Both, courtesy Robert and Eva Mae Merrick.)

The large fireplace with the detailed hand-carved mantel is the showcase in the parlor (above), a simple but eloquently decorated room where family and guests could mingle in front of a fire. The detail in the woodcarvings continues into the upstairs sitting room (below). The large windows let in natural light to highlight the room, making it a perfect hideaway to sit and read a book. The portrait on the right is of Frederick S. Merrick, who was born in the Merrick House Hotel in 1853. He was a prominent 19th-century businessman affiliated with the Standard Horse Nail Company. On the left is a framed photograph of his sons, Frederick Ickes Merrick and Silas Clarence Merrick. The girl in the portrait on the easel is his daughter Marguerite. (Both, courtesy Robert and Eva Mae Merrick.)

The woodwork in the library was made from flamed birch wood. In his youth, Frederick S. Merrick, a talented violinist, was the leader of a theater orchestra. His wife, Clara, also an accomplished musician, had a beautiful soprano voice and was a well-known concert singer before her marriage. The couple passed their love of music to their children. The piano (above) is where their son, Frederick Ickes Merrick, learned to play. The 22-foot-by-15-foot dining room (below) is another of the many showcase rooms in the house. Tiger maple wood was used to construct the built-in mirrored buffets and the floor-to-ceiling fireplace is highlighted with tiles made locally. On the right, a set of pocket doors leads to the butler's pantry. (Both, courtesy Robert and Eva Mae Merrick.)

The New Brighton Optimist little league baseball team posed for this team photograph on August 22, 1955. James Spratt (left) and Robert Beck were the coaches. Billy Maybray (first row, without a hat) went on to become a member of the band The Jaggerz, which formed in 1965. (Photograph by Pete Pavlovic; courtesy J.J. Spratt Funeral Home.)

The Jaggerz included, from left to right, Thom Davies, Donnie Ierace, Benny Faiella, Billy Maybray, Jimmy Ross, and Jim Pugliano. Maybray wrote their hit "(That's Why) Baby I Love You." Another hit was "The Rapper," which went gold in March 1970, when it was the number one song in the country. Fans remember their performances at the high school and on *American Bandstand*. (Courtesy Leslie Maybray Jarovich.)

Six

ABOUT TOWN

This photograph shows the downtown business district on Broadway looking south from Butler Street in 1882, when the main avenue was dirt. When it rained, the streets turned to mud and the only mode of transportation was the horse and buggy. Almost all the establishments had a hitching post out front to accommodate customers. (Courtesy BCHRLF.)

This view of New Brighton was taken from the hillside below Patterson Heights in 1866. In the foreground is the Beaver Division of the Pennsylvania Canal. Many industries took advantage of the waterpower and cheap modes of transporting freight by building factories along the banks of the river. The covered toll bridge on the left took travelers over the Beaver River between New Brighton and Beaver Falls. The town flourished in the early days, when many young entrepreneurs

came to the area. Many opened their establishments downtown on Broadway, including Edwin Marquis, H.T. and J. Reeves, Chamberlin and Cuthbertson, Henry Mendenhall, Milton Marquis, and Benjamin R. Bradford. Along the river, Bentley and Gerwig operated a twine factory, Charles Coal manufactured buckets, tubs, and washboards, and Henry Fisher ran an icehouse. (Photograph by Henry Noss.)

Hiram Reed Sr. stands in front of his house on Broadway near Falls Street in 1856. Reed was a highly respected citizen and a longtime grocery store owner. In 1859, he was elected town constable. He was director of the Beaver County Poor House for a one-year term in 1870. He retired in 1883, turning the successful grocery business over to his son, Hiram Jr.

David Townsend donated three adjoining lots on Bridge Street for public use in 1815. In the early years, the lots were used by carnivals, medicine shows, and for grazing. In 1879, councilman Joseph Wilson cleaned up debris, planted trees, and added gravel walkways, creating what is now Townsend Park. The flag tower stood from 1898 until 1925, when a resident fell to his death and the monument was dismantled.

Edward Dawes employed the R.B. McDanel Company to erect a gymnasium on Allegheny Street in 1929. New Brighton High School graduate and building architect Jesse E. Martsolf was present when Dawes donated the $80,000 brick building and property to the New Brighton School District. The handsome structure (pictured), known as Dawes Gymnasium, was used for high school basketball games, physical education, and other indoor sporting events.

Jesse Martsolf was a well-known architect in the early 1900s. He designed many buildings and churches throughout Beaver County, including Burry's Church, the Beaver County Children's Home annex, Beaver Valley School of Nursing, and Zelienople Orphan's Home. Martsolf designed a memorial and recreation park on property donated by the former owners of the Dawes and Myler factory. The 18-acre recreation area included a playground, a basketball court, softball fields, and tennis courts.

The streetcar tracks are visible in this photograph, which looks north from Thirteenth Street along Penn Avenue toward Oak Hill in 1900. Behind the trees on the right was a structure called the pebble house, which stood at the rear of the property at 1121 Penn Avenue. The house was built entirely of round cobblestones laid in cement by Francis Houlette in 1856. The structure was torn down in 1908.

This photograph shows Fifth Street heading toward Oak Hill in the early 1900s. The stunning mansion in the center, with its stately columns and unique architecture, overlooked the town. The large stone steps and gazebo gave an added elegance to the home. There is no record of when the house was torn down, but the once-pristine hillside yard and stone steps are now overgrown with brush and trees.

This photograph shows Sixth Avenue between Ninth and Tenth Streets in 1894. The Noss family home (on the left, with steps) was the main attraction on this block. Neighbors would sit on their porches and listen as the famous Noss family practiced their musical selections and comedy acts. The once-shady street is now almost void of trees.

Between 1891 and 1899, employers began to decrease work hours and give workers Saturdays off, giving more time for leisure activities. A favorite pastime for the whole family was spending the day on the banks of the Beaver River watching the boat races.

Hundreds gathered to witness the 35-mile automobile race between B.O. Fair's Maxwell and Howard McCreery's Buick in 1909. Word spread that the Buick broke a rear gear and was out of the race, so Steve Moltrup Jr. replaced him with his 60-horsepower Stoddard-Dayton. The Maxwell broke down as soon as the race began; not wanting to disappoint the crowd, Moltrup raced through the town course anyway as if he had a competitor.

Several young girls gather at the starting line to run a footrace at Junction Park in the early 1900s. The winner of the event was 12-year-old Patience Solomon, who was awarded a ribbon and received a free pass to enjoy the amusement park rides for a day.

The Ringling Brothers Barnum and Bailey Circus arrived by train on July 4, 1909. Hundreds of spectators gathered to watch as cages of lions, bears, tigers, and monkeys, as well as 25 elephants, were paraded down Third Avenue. A calliope played as jugglers, 45 acrobats, and snake charmers entertained the crowds on the way to Junction Park, where an afternoon performance attracted more than 10,000 people. (Courtesy BCHRLF.)

The Beaver Valley Traction Company opened Junction Park to the public in July 1901. Officials hoped the park would increase off-hour ridership and spared no expense to make a first-class summer resort. Attractions over the years included a funhouse, a house of horror, amusement rides, harness racing, boxing matches, a baseball field, dinner theater, a dance pavilion, and food booths. Nothing remains of the once-popular park today. (Courtesy BCHRLF.)

A state-of-the-art merry-go-round (above, right) was built at Junction Park in 1909. A calliope played as ornate, hand-carved painted horses took riders around the carousel. The racetrack and grandstand (above, left), surrounded by a picket fence, featured harness races and attracted spectators from the tri-state area. Purses as high as $800 were awarded. Below, fairgoers enjoy Barnum Boss ice cream while relaxing in the shade. Barnum's ice cream was made from pure cream and was the most popular local treat in the early 1900s. Contests were held throughout the summer to see who could eat the most ice cream cones. In 1902, Bernie Templeton amazed the crowd when he consumed 23 ice cream cones in less than four minutes.

The Country Store was a popular booth to visit during the Beaver County Fair, held at Junction Park. Local organizations manned the booths, which sold homemade foods and handmade craft items. Proceeds benefited the Beaver Valley General Hospital fund. The Greystone Gardens Theater (below) was opened at the park in June 1901. Every week, there was a change of bill, attracting acts from all over the world. The Russian Quartet from St. Petersburg, Russia, performed every night for two weeks in 1902, dancing and singing all their native songs. Professor Parker and his famous dogs, Parole and Kata, entertained many sold-out crowds. Vaudeville comedy acts were also popular and performers were booked from the best vaudeville venues in New York. A moving picture show delighted the audience after the live performances.

A three-deck figure-eight roller coaster was built at Junction Park in 1904. Plans were set for a grand opening on July 4, but on June 29, a strong storm accompanied by heavy winds tore through the park, destroying the roller coaster within minutes and leaving a tangled metal mess. The coaster was rebuilt and opened a few months later with free rides, to the delight of the public.

The lemonade stand was another popular booth at Junction Park. Fresh lemons were shipped from Florida to make a thirst-quenching drink for fairgoers. The ladies used ice picks to chip ice off the large blocks supplied by local merchant Fred Duerr. Tall glasses were then filled with ice before the fresh-squeezed lemonade was poured over it. The refreshing drink kept everyone cool on hot summer days.

The dance pavilion at Junction Park opened on June 17, 1901. Midnight dances were very popular events attended mostly by younger crowds. Admission prices were $1.50 for couples and 50¢ for single ladies. The John Philip Sousa band, known for renditions of American military and patriotic marches, played at many functions held in the pavilion. The building was destroyed by fire in 1945.

This photograph, taken around 1925, shows the Alum Rocks in the background and the houses and businesses along the Beaver River. The Alum Rocks were steep, rugged cliffs covered with brush and pines. Sycamore and willow trees jutted out from between the rocks. When the railroad built train tracks along the riverbank, these buildings on the east bank of the river were razed.

Residents look over the damage at Junction Park after the 1907 flood. Spring rains, combined with the melting winter snows, left a wide path of destruction. The roller coaster (right) is half-submerged. The Beaver County Traction Company was forced to suspend all trolley traffic until the water completely receded and the debris was cleared from the tracks.

This photograph was taken outside the Kennedy Keg Works after a flood struck in March 1907. Those leaving the factories told of the swiftness of the current as they tried to get to safety. They described how kegs, logs, driftwood, chicken coops, and even houses were taken quickly downstream. The sign on this building shows the high-water level from the 1884 flood. The keg works was established in 1876.

Here, floodwaters break through the remnants of the old canal in the flood that swept through town in March 1913. The building on the right was the old Blount Hotel, which was operated by innkeeper Francis Blount in the 1860s and later used as a factory. The Sharon Bridge, which crosses the Beaver River between New Brighton and Fallston, was washed away from the force of the swift-moving floodwaters.

Residents who lived in the low-lying areas of town also experienced damage to their houses and belongings during floods. In March 1913, lower Third Avenue was left submerged in water. The frequent floods and high water forced residents to evacuate their homes on many occasions. Despite this, residents always returned when the waters receded and started life all over again.

Pennsylvania & Lake Erie Railroad employees report to work by boat at the freight and passenger station in Fallston, a few days after the 1913 flood. It was more than a week before the water receded enough for workers to clear the tracks of rubble. The train, seen here past the high water full of cargo, was able to leave the station after a 10-day delay. (Courtesy BCHRLF.)

More than 50 homes were flooded and many residents had to be evacuated from their homes by boats as the worst flood in New Brighton's history occurred on St. Patrick's Day 1936. The entire area south of 20th Street was under several feet of water. The muddy Beaver River surged shortly before noon and exceeded the previous high-water marks from 1884, 1907, and 1913.

Seven

EDUCATION AND RELIGION

Local contractor Henry Fetter built the red brick Kenwood School for Boys (left) on Oak Hill in 1855. Headmaster Rev. Joseph P. Taylor described the campus in 1869: "It is in a grove of oaks on elevated grounds. The location is one of singular beauty with more than 40 acres, and affords ample space for outdoor activities." Years later, the entire complex became the Beaver Valley General Hospital.

New Brighton became an independent school district in April 1880 and elected professor John Collier as superintendent. First Ward School opened on January 6, 1890, on Penn Avenue and Pearl Street. The building was purchased by the Church of Christ and renovated in 1945. The congregation decided to erect a new building at the present location and the old school-turned-church was razed in September 1966.

The Junior Red Cross, the youth division of the American Red Cross, was headquartered on Third Avenue near Thirteenth Street. Children were taught what to do during times of natural disasters and learned safeguards to prevent accidents. Members also collected clothes and other necessary items for those devastated by floods or fires. Every Christmas, members received gifts, including the Red Cross dolls and books seen here. (Courtesy J.J. Spratt Funeral Home.)

George Kreuger of Johnstown was awarded the contract to build a high school on the site of the former ladies' seminary on Lock Street. This photograph shows the Central School shortly after its completion in 1893. The 12-classroom building cost $29,700 and was one of Beaver County's largest educational facilities at the time. Central High School opened its doors to students in 1894. After the school was struck by lightning and badly damaged on June 21, 1917, it was repaired quickly and students returned to class within a month. When the new high school on Allegheny Street opened in 1921, Central School became a junior high school and grade school. The school served the town for 80 years before closing it doors in 1973. Below is the third grade class of 1943–1944. (Below, courtesy Vera Herr.)

Kenwood School was an eight-room building constructed in 1912. Students marched out of school to piano music and gathered in the halls on Friday afternoons to sing songs, led by the principal, Lulu Zimmerman. The Penn Avenue building served as an elementary school until 1973 and was razed in June 2012. Miss Solomon's 1957–1958 kindergarten class (below) included, from left to right, (first row) Martha Leopardi, Linda Cooper, Debra Paton, Nancy Spickerman, Larry Grimm, Rob Locke, Sandy Greathouse, and Jeff Majzlik; (second row) Paul Spickerman, Betsy Fry, John Book, David Ketterer, Mary Ann McNees, Fred Sempf, Loraine Herstine, and Debbie Orr; (third row) unidentified, Ralph Rafferty, unidentified, John Lott, John Francona, Bill Rexroad, and unidentified; (fourth row) Carol Lambert, Richard Operhall, unidentified, Jeff Pilchard, unidentified, and Paul Long. (Below, photograph by Bob Correll, courtesy Rex and Doris Rexroad.)

The Kenwood School's first-grade class in 1960–1961 included, from left to right, (first row) Bonnie Hogue, Barbara Barnes, Richard Greathouse, Greg Bork, Jeff Rylott, Karen Chaney, Vicki Smarsh, and Glen Rivoland; (second row) Ron Best, Kathy Anderson, Sharon Spickerman, Gretchen Spickerman, Carolyn McNeese, Gary Pasquale, and Tommy Butler; (third row) Jane Miller, Harry Beitsch, Martha Emert, Steve Crouse, Billy Lilly, and Tom Volenic; (fourth row) Becky Lott, Ron Radcliffe, John Volenic, Kenny Lane, Cindy Sprecker, and Jim Deane. Lulu Zimmerman was a teacher as well as being the school's longtime principal. The students above were part of the last graduating class at the old high school on Allegheny Street in 1973. Catherine Holtzman's 1962–1963 third-grade class is below. (Photographs by Bob Correll; below, courtesy Rex and Doris Rexroad.)

Third Ward School (above) was designed by architect A. Koehler and was formally opened on November 31, 1882. The first principal was Mary Graham. Below, the fire department visits the kindergarten class in 1957 to discuss fire safety. The students are, from left to right, (first row) teacher Miss Hamilton, Connie Smith, Frank Muccic, Vickie Owens, Karen Mooney, George Chambers, John Turcic, Donald Cook, Bonnie Mae Enke, Patty Capo, Mary Jean Yaria, Karen Keefer, Bonnie Boswell, Sharon Kittle, Susan Bell, Mary Lynn Ondrusek, and Alice Lowery; (second row) Isabelle Keibler, John Lack, George Maze, Debra Banyas, and Sally Stitt; (third row) teacher Helen Druschel, Thomas Miladin, Terry Russo, Robert Bump, John Basile, Edward Spratt, Richard Falen, Harry White, Jack Keith, and Robert Corfield; (fourth row) Gregory Snowden, David Seery, Keith Parkinson, Joseph McKelvey, Woody Benson, and Jack Mulik. (Courtesy Connie Smith.)

St. Joseph Church started a school in the church basement in 1884. The Sisters of St. Joseph, who devoted their time to a teaching ministry, arrived to assist parish priest Rev. Joseph Bingham in organizing the school. Early teachers were Sister Elizabeth Coleman, Sister Loyola Hayes, Sister Cyril Fowler, and Sister Evangelist Finan. The St. Joseph School building (above) was erected in 1922 at the corner of Seventh Avenue and Sixth Street. The red brick structure housed children in grades one through eight until its doors closed in 1973. The building was then used for Confraternity of Christian Doctrine (CCD) classes and church functions until September 1994, when the building was razed to make room for a parking lot. The image below is a look inside the fifth-grade classroom at the St. Joseph School in 1955. Sister Linus was the teacher. (Courtesy Father Tom Kredel.)

The 1948 sixth-grade class at St. Joseph School poses on the front steps for this class photograph. At the time, boys walked to the high school once a week to attend shop class. Ninth-grade students were transferred to the New Brighton Junior High School on Penn Avenue before going on to high school. (Courtesy Etta Labon Moldovan.)

The cornerstone was laid for the new S.S. Cyril and Methodius Church and School on lower Third Avenue on January 20, 1957. The building was dedicated on September 14, 1957. The parish merged with St. Joseph Church in 1994 to form the Holy Family Parish. The 1939 second-grade class from S.S. Cyril and Methodius School is seen here. (Courtesy Mimi Ondrusek.)

The Maypole dance was first performed here on May 1, 1905. Dancers held crepe-paper ribbons attached to a pole as the graceful dance set to music began with the inner circle going right and the outer circle going left. They then alternated by going under the ribbon of the first girl, over the ribbon of the next, and so on, creating a weaving pattern down the pole.

William Bierer was the band director for many years at the New Brighton Junior High School. The band is seen here during the 1964–1965 school year. The 181-member band showed off its talents at the annual music festival held in the school auditorium and marched in all the local parades, with drum major Pam Jannuzi leading the way. (Photograph by Bob Correll; courtesy Rex and Doris Rexroad.)

The cornerstone for the high school was laid at the corner of Allegheny Street and Tenth Avenue in 1919. Students began classes at the new school in September 1921. The three-story brick building had 21 rooms, administrative offices, and an auditorium with a balcony and stage. The 52-year-old school closed its doors in 1973. Today, the building houses the E.B. McNitt apartments for senior citizens.

The 1934 New Brighton High School football team ended its season with a 20-6 win over the Beaver Falls Tigers, the second consecutive year the Lions defeated their rival. Weather conditions were not favorable and players contended with muddy, icy fields at most games. Coach George Roark led the Lions to five wins, two losses, and a tie that year. Ollie Molter was team captain. (Photograph by Graule Studio.)

Quarterback Bill Edwards guided the Lions varsity squad to a 29-6 win over Butler High School in the 1945 season opener. The team's seniors were Edwards, John Ellis, Wilfred Rawl, Richard Sylvester, Dale Fortune, Raul Tucker, Earl Garen, Albert Peluso, Eddy Haddox, and Frank Budiscak. The coaches were George Roark and Melvin Miller. The players ended the season with seven wins, one loss, and a tie. (Courtesy J.J. Spratt Funeral Home.)

In no particular order, Ruth Capo, Mary Lou Perrott, Helen Klutka, Margaret Lazar, Jean Mittner, and Mildred Leimer were New Brighton High School majorettes in 1946. They twirled at football games, in area parades, and at concerts held in the park. Richard Fleming was the band director at the time. (Courtesy BCHRLF.)

The offense of the 1950 New Brighton High School football team posed for this photograph before the Western Pennsylvania Interscholastic Athletic League (WPIAL) championship game against Canonsburg. They are, from left to right, (first row) Jack Grimm, Jon Best, Joe Dwyer, George Majors, Don Snowberger, Frank Chufe, and Don Moore; (second row) Eddie Moldovan, Kenneth Majors, Jack Dyson, and Costel Denson. James Myers and John (Tito) Francona are not pictured. (Courtesy Eddie Moldovan Sr.)

Eddie Moldovan (22) fends off Canonsburg players on a four-yard run in the third quarter of the championship game at Dormont High School in November 1950. Canonsburg's Sam Karavolias comes up from the secondary to make the tackle while Jim Malone (42) lends a hand. The Lions' Jack Dyson (23) gets set to block out Canonsburg's Wayne Edmonds. (Courtesy Eddie Moldovan Sr.)

Umpire Art French signals a touchdown as the New Brighton High School cheerleaders jump with delight at the 1950 championship game. Halfback Eddie Moldovan is on the ground after smashing through a Canonsburg tackle at the two-yard line. Coach Charles Buzard's protégés did not disappoint that day, as the exciting playoff game ended in a 12-12 tie and New Brighton and Canonsburg shared the WPIAL championship title. (Courtesy Eddie Moldovan Sr.)

The 1951 May Court included, from left to right, (first row) Shirley Bodner, Joanne Brown, Eleanor Straile, Joanne Shields, Alyce Enke, Betty Kolumban, Joan Cornelius, Frances Swaney, Nancy Butler, and Alice Fleming; (second row) Philip Feit, William McDowell, George Grecich, Eddie Moldovan, Jack Dyson, Peggy Hogue, queen Lee Harris, scepter bearer Joanne Taggart, Philip Bross, Ronald Blackburn, Fred Riddle, Ralph Householder, and Robert Williams. The heralds on either end are Jeanne Pasquale (left) and Susie Hamilton.

The New Brighton High School basketball team captured the 1951 WPIAL section nine championship under coach Melvin Miller. The Lions beat the Beaver Bobcats by a score of 49-47. The team included, from left to right, (first row) George Banyas, Kenneth Majors, Abe Preston, William Beck, and Robert Williams; (second row) Joseph Dwyer, Donald Snowberger, Jack Grimm, Ray Tannehill, Jack Dyson, and John (Tito) Francona. (Courtesy Eddie Moldovan Sr.)

Rudolph takes a quick nap in his small house as Santa and his reindeer land on the lawn of the high school on Allegheny Street in this 1953 Christmas display. For many years, under the direction of manual training instructor Ivan N. Coene, students spent their class time cutting out and assembling these elaborate displays. Mildred Pratt's art students assisted with painting the displays.

Rev. Alonzo Potter laid the cornerstone of the Christ Episcopal Church on March 27, 1851. The first pastor was Rev. William Paddock. This photograph from June 7, 1919, shows the beautiful English-style church decorated by parishioners to help the town welcome the soldiers coming home from war. This church building is the oldest in New Brighton.

Below, hundreds gathered to witness the cornerstone laying of the Methodist Episcopal Church on the corner of Lock and Front Streets on September 12, 1866. When the church was almost completed, a strong storm struck on July 3, 1867, blowing down three walls to the first-floor windows. Rev. James McIllyar convinced the congregation to rebuild. (Courtesy BCGHC.)

Billy Sunday was the first baseball player to run the bases in 14 seconds, in the 1880s. He gave up his baseball career and converted to evangelical Christianity. This photograph looks across the river from Fallston, showing the tents set up for one of the many revivals he held here in the early 1900s. His energetic preaching style drew thousands of people eager to hear him speak. (Courtesy J.J. Spratt Funeral Home.)

The cornerstone for the St. Joseph Roman Catholic Church was laid on November 17, 1871. Parishioners worshipped in the basement until funds were secured to finish the building in 1875. Father Michael Ryan (inset) was the parish priest when the church burned in 1911. Today, the church is on Seventh Avenue and is known as the Holy Family Parish; Father Tom Kredel now presides over the Catholic community he grew up in.

A fire devastated the St. Joseph Roman Catholic Church on October 25, 1911. Mary O'Hara, Father Ryan's housekeeper, first spotted the flames. The fire was started in the sacristy by a candle left burning, which soon set fire to nearby tapestries. Firemen had to break in a rear door to gain entrance to the church. Firefighter Harry Knauff sustained a fractured left shoulder when he fell through the floor into the basement. Due to the valiant efforts of the firemen, the church was saved from total loss. The photograph below shows the damage in the sanctuary. This was the second time the parish lost a church building to fire. The previous church, located on the same site, burned to the ground in 1876.

First Communion is considered one of the holiest and most important occasions in a Catholic's life. Children receive first communion when they are seven or eight years old. Father Regis Hannon (left) and Sister Mary Jerome are seen here with the communion class of 1963. Many of these students were later part of the last graduating class at the old high school on Allegheny Street in 1973. (Courtesy J.J. Spratt Funeral Home.)

Board members from the Marion Hill Christian and Missionary Alliance Church in 1975 included, from left to right, (first row) Gene Schuab, Roger Smith, Roy Pander, Ruth Bingham, Rev. Clyde Davis, Robert Clemens, and Howard Bowen; (second row) Bart Eakles, Thomas Young, Pearl Rinard, Andrew Ketterer, Boyd Ketterer, Rev. Leroy Kennedy, and Harry Rader; (third row) Edward Robitz, Art Sheets, and Lee Holt. (Courtesy Art Sheets.)

The United Presbyterian Church was between the Beaver County Trust Bank and Christner's Bible Bookstore on Third Avenue. The first church service held here was in 1886. Early pastors were Rev. J.D. Glenn, Rev. A. Wallace, Dr. W. Barr, Rev. Robert Hay, Rev. Clarence Williamson, Rev. William Rotzler, Rev. Joseph Vandervort, Rev. A. Spotts, Rev. T. Spotts, Reverend Gordon, Reverend Brightwell, and Rev. William Lane. A fire destroyed the church and the neighboring bookstore on October 20, 1963. The congregation purchased property on Oak Hill and a new church was erected.

The steeple is lifted onto the new Westminster United Presbyterian Church at 115 North Mercer Road in Oak Hill on October 16, 1964. The congregation held its first church service in this location on December 11, 1964, with the Rev. Ronald Moslener presiding. (Courtesy BCGHC.)

The Methodist Episcopal congregation purchased the lot at the corner of Eleventh Street and Sixth Avenue in 1901 for $1,700. The handsome brick church above was dedicated on January 20, 1904, with services by Rev. A.J. Ashe. It later became the First United Methodist Church. Charles Bestwick and Carrie Johnson donated the church bell in memory of their mother, Sarah Bestwick, a longtime church member, on April 4, 1920. Members of the First United Methodist Church choir (below) included, from left to right, (first row) Christine VanKirk, unidentified, Doris Rexroad, Betty McNeese, Lulabelle Beagle, Mildred Veiock, Pauline Weles, JoAnne Willis, unidentified, Betty Forsythe, Evelyn McNees, Ms. Redmond, and Tina Kelbaugh; (second row) Carl McNees, Dr. Robert Phillips, Lester Veiock, Roy Kelbaugh, unidentified, William Rexroad Sr., and choir director Lauren McCaughtry. (Below, courtesy Rex and Doris Rexroad.)

Eight

ORGANIZATIONS

Boy Scouts salute as scoutmaster David Mendenhall raises the flag in this 1914 photograph. The organization held meetings in a room above the Autenreith store on Third Avenue. The scouts camped out twice a month during the summer at Daugherty Woods, outside New Brighton. They learned outdoor skills through a variety of activities, including hiking, cooking over a campfire, and team competitions.

Members of the Ladies Benevolent Association, a Quaker society founded in January 1846, are seen here in an undated photograph. The group was organized to help the destitute survive the cold winters. They provided warm clothing, shoes, and other necessities to all in need. The first officers were president Elizabeth Martin, vice president Elizabeth Blake, and secretary and treasurer Amanda Dutcher. The 131-year-old organization disbanded in 1977.

Lincoln Club members march in the 1899 Memorial Day parade. The group organized as the Wide Awakes in 1856, and changed its name to the Lincoln Club in 1880. William Fetter organized a drum and fife corps on July 2, 1881. The club entertained parade crowds with torchlight processions, unique political banners waving on long poles, and musical selections. They were the oldest Republican marching club in the United States.

Mary Taggert was the inspiration behind the formation of the Woman's Christian Temperance Union, organized in 1881. Her spirit and ability to connect with young people was one of her greatest strengths and it helped guide them toward a life of education and religious teachings. The organization rented a room in the Blount Building, where a library was established so adolescents could enjoy an evening of social activities without alcohol.

The New Brighton Concert Band, under the direction of Louis Morrow, delights an audience at the Empire Theater on Third Avenue around 1927. They also performed at all the games played by the Damascus Steel baseball team. Ollie Molter was the band manager for many years.

This photograph shows members of the Oak Leaf Camp No. 5873 of the Modern Woodmen of America in their meeting room above the Butler and Jackson clothing store in 1909. The group was chartered on January 11, 1901, with members Dr. Harry Coyle, M.K. Bebout, R.M. Bevington, William Carr, F.B. Golden, William Kilgore, Beroni Mahon, Terrance McBreen, George McCoy, David Sutherland, Charles McGaffick, James Staley, David Thomas, and George Trover.

The International Order of Rainbow for Girls, New Brighton Assembly No. 58, installed new officers on June 2, 1966. They are, from left to right, (first row) Judy Sines, Ardys Mitsch, worthy advisor Nancy Greco, Beth Fezell, Lynnette Bowser, and Jayne Eggensberger; (second row) Margie Yoho, Connie Smith, Laura Roser, Arla Mitsch, Karen Roser, Bonnie Henry, and mother advisor Alice Stillwagon; (third row) Louise Sherrill, Shirley Brewer, Cheryl Bork, unidentified, Karen Mason, and two unidentified. (Courtesy Connie Smith.)

The Beaver County YMCA was organized in 1889. For many young people, the YMCA was a second home, providing social and physical activities. Youngsters were inspired to make choices based on Christian principles in order to strengthen themselves and the community. This four-story brick structure on the corner of Third Avenue at Eighth Street was built in 1915. It was a modern facility with a first-floor gymnasium complete with a basketball court and a running track, reading rooms, offices, and a reception area. The basement contained a swimming pool, locker rooms, and a boy's game room. The top floors were rented as sleeping rooms. A.O. Ludwig was hired as general director of the new facilities. Below, 58 boys attended the annual holiday overnight encampment in the gymnasium on December 30, 1947. (Both, courtesy YMCA.)

The first organized college basketball game played in the United States was on April 8, 1893, between the YMCA and Geneva College. Peach baskets were used instead of hoop baskets and Geneva won 3-0. The 1899 YMCA basketball team included, from left to right, (first row) physical director Harry David, John Kelley, and Ray Bain; (second row) Billy Baker, Bill Greaves, Harvey Russell, and Dave Creighton. (Courtesy YMCA.)

The YMCA hosted its first gymnasium exhibition to a packed house in 1930. This boys' group, which demonstrated 12 different pyramids, was the highlight of the show. Other events included tumbling demonstrations, parallel bar drills, badminton matches, marching drills, and a basketball game. The day ended with a family picnic held in the YMCA dining room. The presentation was so popular that it became an annual event. (Courtesy YMCA.)

In December 1944, the annual older boys YMCA and Hi-Y conference was held in the auditorium of the Grace Methodist Church on Sixth Street. James C. Mace from the Pittsburgh YMCA was the keynote speaker. Over 100 families responded when the call went out to house the 257 boys attending. School superintendent E.B. McNitt and burgess Tom Bishop welcomed delegates at the opening banquet. (Courtesy YMCA.)

YMCA camp leaders are seen here at Camp Kon-o-Kee in June 1950. The counselors oversaw 210 children during the popular two-week summer camp, which the YMCA has hosted since 1926. The campers were separated into age groups and assigned cabins for their stay. Fun-filled days included swimming, fishing, and hiking. At night, campers enjoyed sing-a-longs and storytelling around the campfire. (Courtesy YMCA.)

Some of the most important people at the YMCA camp were the mothers and grandmothers who volunteered their time to make three nutritious meals a day for camp attendees. Above, the cooks prepare meatloaf, mashed potatoes and gravy, vegetables, and dessert for an evening meal in 1949. The photograph below shows the YMCA camp cooks reunion held in 1965. The deserving volunteers were treated to a catered meal as they reminisced about the days spent in the camp kitchen, peeling 100 pounds of potatoes, cooking 50 pounds of roast beef for Sunday dinners, and turning 25 pounds of navy beans into a delicious soup. At the end of the evening, each woman received a red carnation and a thank-you from YMCA director L.H. McCullough. (Both, courtesy YMCA.)

In 1902, the rented rooms above Albert G. Harvey's grocery on Third Avenue housed the first armory of Company B, 110th Infantry state militia. Five years later, the armory moved to a building on Second Avenue. Martsolf Brothers secured the bid to construct a new armory on the old Fombelle property on upper Third Avenue in 1908. The cost of the building and property totaled $27,000. Maj. Harry Cuthbertson placed a copper box filled with company memorabilia in the cornerstone on September 17, 1908. The armory was formally dedicated on May 1, 1909, with prominent men in civil and military life attending, including Gov. Edwin Stuart. The armory was abandoned in 1978 and Company B moved to Chippewa. Today, the building houses the New Brighton municipal offices. The inside of the armory is seen below in 1909. (Above, courtesy BCGHC.)

This photograph, taken on August 29, 1899, shows the welcome home banner erected on Broadway at Falls Street. The following morning, the largest parade in New Brighton's history was viewed by 20,000 people, who had all gathered to honor returning soldiers. Maj. Harry Cuthbertson, Capt. John Sherwood, and Lt. Col. James Barnett led the troops as they marched through the banner to the cheers of the grateful crowds. (Courtesy Robert and Eva Mae Merrick.)

Returning soldiers march through the banner in 1919 after spending two years at war. The celebration was bittersweet, as several soldiers gave up their lives while fighting in France and many more were wounded. Though the men were applauded for their success, the outbreaks of cheering in previous celebrations was lacking due to the knowledge that some of the families present had lost a loved one in the war.

Every storefront in town was decorated in red, white, and blue. "Welcome Home" banners and American flags graced the downtown business district in preparation for the parade on June 7, 1919. New Brighton continues to honor fallen soldiers every Memorial Day with a parade. Residents have answered the call to duty and have faithfully served their country from the Civil War through the Afghanistan War. (Courtesy BCHRLF.)

Military trucks line the entire length of Third Avenue while a company of soldiers stopped in New Brighton on March 17, 1918. The visiting unit enjoyed a hot meal with members of Company B in the armory. Since there was not enough gasoline in town to fuel all the trucks to capacity, each vehicle received half a tank of gas before heading out to New Castle.

The New Brighton Fire Department started a hook and ladder brigade, known as Company Six, in 1894. Here, an unidentified fireman shows off the company's first hook and ladder truck at Junction Park. It took one man to drive the truck and another to run the hoses. In its first year, the hook and ladder brigade helped the department put out 15 fires.

A gas explosion severely damaged George Hartman's home on Sixth Avenue on March 10, 1902. Minnie Hartman was engulfed in flames after she struck the match that ignited the blast and George was blown across the dining room and through a double door. Minnie recovered after a long hospital stay. In 1909, while battling a blaze at Sherwood Pottery, George Hartman, a well-known firefighter from Hose Company One, was fatally injured.

Some type of fire department has served New Brighton since 1838, when James Erwin and Septimus Dunlap built the first hose house at Broadway and Falls Street. The department was known as the Jefferson Fire Company. A second department was organized as the Mechanics Fire Department in 1859. The department's fire apparatuses consisted of four hose carts, one in the center of each ward. A department was formed with four companies and 32 men in 1893 and eventually became known as the New Brighton Volunteer Fire Department. Above, members of the 1925 New Brighton Fire Department Company Four pose around their truck. Below, members of the 1925 New Brighton Fire Department Company Two pose in front of their stationhouse. They are, from left to right, Lester R. Jackson, Lewis Boettner, Harry W. Matheny, Carl McNees, Clarence Henry, George Cleckner, Frank Mittner, and William Merriman.

The New Brighton Cemetery Association held a meeting on July 12, 1858, regarding the establishment of a town cemetery. Rev. Joseph P. Taylor was elected acting chairman with R.E. Hoopes as secretary. Members voted to purchase a 32-acre tract of land adjoining Blockhouse Run. A charter was drawn up with the name Grove Cemetery and was presented to the Pennsylvania General Assembly for approval. The cemetery was dedicated on October 13, 1859, with Reverend

Taylor presiding over the ceremony. At the time, lots sold for $40 each. William Shaffer was the first sexton, receiving $20 per month plus free rent to live in the cottage near the cemetery entrance. According to cemetery records, employees were paid 90¢ per day. Drivers of the horse and cart received $1.50 per day. This photograph was taken in 1890.

The volunteer Pulaski Township Fire Department incorporated in 1927. The department started as a state-supported forest-firefighting unit in the early 1900s. In the 1940s photograph above, members included, from left to right, (first row) Glen Sheets, Donald Shaffer, three unidentified men, Stewart Sinclair, C. Klitz, Les Reynolds, William Kocher, and unidentified; (second row) Tate Kuhl, Charles Higby, unidentified, Michael Chufe, Leland Peters, Wade Hoffman, and Sullivan Pasquale. Below, the Pulaski Township Ladies Auxiliary posed for a photograph on June 30, 1950. The members are, from left to right, (first row) Lucille Gilliland, Ethelyn Barr, Mabel Reynolds, Mrs. Hartley, Mary Zilk, Mrs. Wherry, Catherine Lane, Catherine Pasquale, Florence Hildebrand, Mrs. Sinclair, Ann Taylor, and Dorothy Higby; (second row) Margaret Reynolds, Wilda Hall, Margaret Sayres, Mary Kuhl, Mae Colwell, Lena Chupe, Louise Higby, and Annie Clark. (Both, courtesy Betty Margetic.)

Nine

DAUGHERTY TOWNSHIP

Daugherty Township residents met with attorney Joseph Tritschler to organize a fire department on June 20, 1952. Charles Anderson and the Goldbertson family donated land for a station on Marion Hill Road. The first truck purchased was a 1953 Ford. The department celebrated its 20-year anniversary in 1972. These firemen are, from left to right, Ron Goldbertson, Morgan Thomas, Donald Stuber, John Tritschler, Fritz Jack, and George Eiler. (Courtesy Sarah Eiler.)

In 1892, attorney Edward B. Daugherty petitioned the court to divide the township on behalf of the Pulaski Township residents. The petition was granted on January 27, 1894. The court ordered that the northern and northeastern parts of Pulaski be designated as Daugherty Township in honor of Edward Black Daugherty, the grandson of Edward Daugherty and John Black, two of the four original Irish Catholic pioneers who settled here in the 1790s.

This photograph was taken on what is now Gulbransen Heights in 1874. From left to right are (first row) Henry Coyle and Alice Coyle; (second row) Patrick Coyle, Mary Ann Daugherty Coyle, family patriarch Daniel M. Daugherty, Daniel D. Daugherty, and Alice M. Daugherty. The house, owned by Patrick and Mary Ann Daugherty Coyle, was near the site of the log cabin built by Edward Daugherty in 1797.

The Watt house (left), off of Helbling Road, is a four-room fieldstone house built by Irish immigrants. Hand-hewn timber beams are still visible in the basement, where the family first lived. When Hugh Watt inherited the 130-acre farm in 1841, he started building two upper levels. Stone fireplaces heated the structure. The house, the oldest in the township, was completed in 1851. The Helbling family has owned the farm since 1935.

The Hoey homestead was originally a log house and was purchased by Robert and Elizabeth Hoey around 1880. When Hoey died in 1885, his wife and children continued to farm the land. Seen here around 1900 are, from left to right, Robert Jr., Elizabeth, John, and Katie Hoey. Note that the logs had been covered with clapboards by this point. The farm was deeded to Harvey and Helen Klein Hoey in 1957. (Courtesy Nancy Hoey Heberling.)

Charles and Margaret Klein pose with their children on their 160-acre farm. The brick homestead was built in 1883 for $3,000. Klein hosted tractor demonstrations there in the early 1900s. The popular events gave local farmers the opportunity to test drive a Fordson tractor and other farm machinery new to the market. The Klein farm had a cider press, an outdoor kitchen, a barn, and a butcher shop. (Courtesy Nancy Hoey Heberling.)

Several hundred relatives and friends attended the first double wedding held in the 100-year history of Burry's Church on June 16, 1934. Helen Klein (left) wed Harvey Hoey, and her older sister, Marguerite Klein, married Elmer Goehring. A wedding dinner was held at the church following the services. The Hoeys enjoyed 61 years together, and the Goehrings were wed for 62 years. (Courtesy Nancy Hoey Heberling.)

A one-room schoolhouse was built on present-day Tulip Drive near Helbling Road in 1872. When a larger building was needed in 1896, the township purchased the Muntz property, on Dogwood Drive, for $100. A frame schoolhouse was constructed and became the Point Pleasant School. Above, students pose outside in 1915. Below, Point Pleasant School students in 1937 included, from left to right, (first row) Fred Budde, Andrew Ketterer, Jack Yeager, unidentified, Steve Markovich, Irvin Miller, unidentified, and Joseph Tice; (second row) Ruth Rombold, Wilda Budde, June Dyson, Elizabeth Teets, Ruth Yeager, Betty Rombold, Richard Householder, Fred Rombold, and Frank Fabyanic; (third row) James Dyson, Theron Ketterer, Norman Rombold, Grace Teets, Mary Rombold, Mary Fabyanic, Michael Markovich, unidentified, Kenneth Householder, Steven Fabyanic, and unidentified; (fourth row) teacher Helen Hoey. (Both, courtesy Nancy Hoey Heberling.)

The students in the undated photograph above were from the one-room Bran Hill School on Mercer Road. Early teachers were Miss Brandt, Mabel Adams, and Miss Rayburn. The schoolhouse closed in 1931 after the Thompson School was built across the road to replace it. Below, former teachers from the Bran Hill School joined 60 students as they honored teacher Mabel Adams Wise on August 24, 1963, at a reunion dinner held at the Daugherty Township fire hall. Adams taught at the school for 50 years before her retirement. Other teachers who attended the dinner included, from left to right, (first row) Ruth Wilson Beighley, Gabe Thompson, Charles Petuch, and Rose Petuch Peluso; (second row) Earl Phillis, Howard Wise, Fernand Tool, Howard Stuber, Louis Klein, and Lee Wise. (Below, courtesy Nancy Hoey Heberling.)

The Daugherty Township school directors advertised for bids to erect a two-room schoolhouse in June 1921. The directors voted unanimously to build the new school using local brick that was readily available and affordable. The Brookdale School opened on Blockhouse Run Road in September 1921. This photograph was taken on June 10, 1925, with teacher Elizabeth Young and her students. The schoolhouse closed due to dwindling attendance in 1941. (Courtesy Sarah Lowe Eiler.)

Vivian Cleis (second from left) poses with her classmates at Brewer School in this undated photograph. The large two-room brick schoolhouse (background) replaced the nearby Brandt School, which was also located off of Route 68. Brewer School opened in the fall of 1929 with 82 students. The school auxiliary helped raise the needed funds for textbooks, supplies, library books, and a piano. (Courtesy BCHRLF.)

Homer Madory, a well-known mail carrier, owned this farm on Silver Springs Road in the mid-1900s. His brother Arthur used the barn (left) to bottle milk for his dairy business in Beaver Falls. George and Sarah Eiler purchased the farm in 1956 and raised two daughters there. George dreamed of building a golf course at the farm but passed away before he could make the project a reality. (Courtesy Sarah Lowe Eiler.)

A group of boys take a break while hiking in Daugherty Woods in 1891. The men in the back were reportedly transient gypsies, who told the boys' fortunes and swapped horses with other visitors until police arrived, stopped the activities, and escorted the gypsies out of town. The woods, on the property of pioneer Edward Daugherty, were a place where locals went to camp, hike, and participate in social activities.

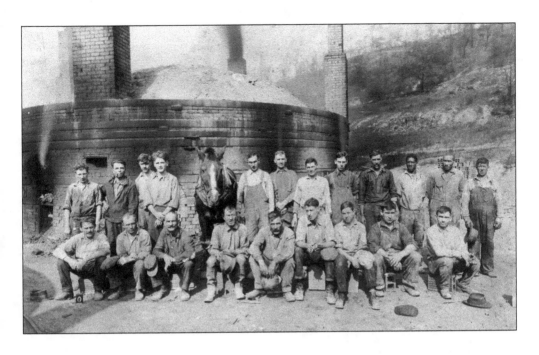

Above, Sewer Pipe Works employees pose in front of one of several beehive-shaped kilns around 1925. In the early days, horses were used to pull wagons loaded with shale from the nearby hills. The shale was ground and sifted into a fine powder and mixed with water to form soft clay, which was forced down through an extruder into a die to form the products, and then fired in a kiln for between 50 and 140 hours. The factory produced a wide range of sewer and drain tile. Below, Sewer Pipe Works personnel pose in front of the products they made at the factory on Blockhouse Run Road. George W. Lowe is on crutches in the back row. He broke his ankle in a work-related accident. (Both, courtesy Sarah Lowe Eiler.)

Visit us at
arcadiapublishing.com

CPSIA information can be obtained
at www.ICGtesting.com
Printed in the USA
LVHW022231160723
752644LV00007B/81